BRAYLEY'S HISTORY OF EWELL
compiled by
John W. Brown

LOCAL HISTORY REPRINTS
316 Green Lane, Streatham, London SW16 3AS

Text originally published in 1878 by
Virtue and Company Ltd
as part of
A Topographical History of Surrey
by
Edward Wedlake Brayley
revised and edited by
Edward Walford

This editon published in 1996 by
Local History Reprints
316 Green Lane
Streatham
London SW16 3AS

ISBN 1 85699 093 1

Cover illustration:
Map of Ewell and the surrounding area c. 1862
being approximately the midway date
between the publication of the first edition
of "A Topographical History of Surrey" in 1848
and the second edition in 1878

INTRODUCTION

Edward Brayley was born in Lambeth in 1773. Following his schooling he became apprenticed to one of London's most famous enamellists, and on completion of his training was employed by Henry Bone to prepare enamel plates for him to paint on. It was whilst still an apprentice that Edward met John Britton, a young man two years his junior, who was apprenticed to his uncle, a tavern keeper in Clerkenwell. The two men, sharing a common interest in the arts and literature, soon struck up a close friendship which was to endure for the following 65 years, and was to result in the publication of various topographical books for which they were both to became famous.

Their partnership had humble beginnings and commenced with a popular song written by Brayley called "The Powder Tax". Britton would perform the song to drum up sales and must have had a flair for the task as up to 80,000 copies were sold. However, the friends soon turned from writing music to writing topographical books. Their first joint venture was the "Beauties of Wiltshire" which Britton wrote with Edward's help for the publishers Vernor & Hood. Britton then persuaded Hood to back them as joint-editors of a series of books called "The Beauties of England and Wales". In June 1800 the two colleagues embarked on collecting material for their new work.

In April 1801 the first volume on Bedfordshire was published. This was quickly followed by books covering Berkshire and Buckinghamshire. By the time the first six volumes had been produced the authors claimed to have trekked up to 3,500 miles in quest of material for their publications.

Although both men were joint editors of the work, it was mainly written by Edward Brayley, with Britton concentrating on conducting correspondence and gathering source material from which the text could be compiled. Writing of his friend, Britton says "Mr. Brayley was constitutionally of a healthy and hardy frame, and was thus enabled to endure and surmount great bodily as well as mental exertion. I have known him to walk 50 miles in one day, and continue the same for three successive days. After completing this labour, from Chester to London, he dressed and spent the evening at a party!"

Brayley was under intense pressure to produce copy for what was in effect a part work with chapters being published each month. Not surprisingly sometimes the instalments fell into arrears, despite the fact that Brayley often worked for up to 16 hours at a stint with a damp handkerchief tied round his head for relief.

Sadly Hood died in 1811, and in January 1812 the major backing for the work was supplied by John Harris, who prior to Hood's death was only a minor backer for the project.

By early 1814 it became obvious that the change of ownership had increased the pressures on Brayley and a rift had developed between him and Harris. With his health failing, Edward withdrew from the venture mid-way through the preparation of the second London volume and the series, which eventually grew to comprise 25 volumes, was completed in 1818 by various other authors.

Whilst writing the "Beauties of England and Wales" Brayley also commenced publishing other popular topographical books and quickly became established as one of the country's leading topographical authors, a position he was to hold for over 50 years.

Relieved of the pressures of having to produce monthly instalments for the "Beauties" he was able to concentrate on these other publications, and for the rest of his life a steady stream of books poured from his pen. Recognition of his achievements came in 1823 when he was elected a fellow of the Society of Antiquaries.

His last work was a mammoth history on the county of Surrey comprising 5 volumes, which, with the exception of the geological section, he wrote between the ages of 68 and 76. Called "A Topographical History of the County of Surrey" it presented a wealth of information in an easy to read format. Brayley updated and broadened the earlier histories of the County, particularly that written by Manning and Bray at the turn of the 19th century. Such was the popularity of the work, the original volumes, published between 1841 and 1848, were revised and updated by Edward Walford and republished in four volumes in 1878.

It is the Ewell section of the second edition issued in 1878 that is reproduced here. It has been necessary to make some minor changes to the text and to slightly rearrange the order in which it appears to accommodate the revised layout of this reprint. Various subheadings have also been included, which did not appear in the original work, to assist the reader when referring to the text.

On 23rd September 1854, five years after completing "A Topographical History of the County of Surrey", Brayley died aged 81.

JOHN W. BROWN

EWELL

This parish borders on that of Maldon on the north, on Cheam on the east, on Banstead on the south, and on Epsom on the south west. Its ancient name was *Ætwelle*, or *Etwel, i.e.* At Well, from its situation at the head of a small stream which runs to Kingston, where it enters the Thames.

The parish of Ewell was enclosed in 1801. There were then reckoned to be 1,238 acres of old enclosure, 707 acres of common land, and 495 acres of waste land. The area of the parish is now computed at 2,437 acres.

EWELL MARKET

A weekly market was held at Ewell in the middle of the seventeenth century, but the date of the charter granting that privilege is not known. Formerly a small market-house stood at the intersection of the roads to London and Kingston, but it was pulled down for the purpose of widening the road.

HOG'S MILL RIVER

Near this site rises a strong spring of beautifully clear water, which soon forms a stream called Hog's Mill River. It abounds with trout, and on its way to Kingston turns several mills.

THE RAILWAY

This place has now the advantage of a railway, a branch from the Croydon line, and terminating at Epsom. The station is about half a mile to the south of the town. There is also a railway station on the Wimbledon and Leatherhead branch of the South-Western line, about the same distance north of the town.

EWELL CASTLE

Ewell castle, the seat of Augustus William Gadesden, Esq., was erected in 1814, on the site of an old house. The mansion is castellated, having octagonal turrets at the angles, and embattled parapets.

On the north side, adjoining the high-road, is an entrance porch leading into a spacious hall, surmounted by a groined ceiling, and lighted by a pointed-arch and mullioned window. The principal front is on the south.

In the pleasure grounds (a portion of which once formed a part of Nonsuch Park) is the site of the old banqueting-house, said to have been built by Henry VIII. About half an acre of land, raised and walled round, with bastions at the corners, marks the spot. The walls were discovered, and some additions made, towards the end of the last century, by Mr. Thomas Calverley, a former owner.

An adjoining field has been designated Diana's Dyke, from having contained a cold bath, traditionally used by Queen Elizabeth, with statues of Diana and Actæon.

ROMAN CONNECTIONS

The probability of Ewell having been occupied as a Roman town, though under some other appellation, has been corroborated by recent discoveries, of which an account, accompanied with drawings by Mr. Archer, was communicated to the Society of Antiquaries in November, 1847, by H. W. Diamond, Esq., F.S.A.

That gentleman superintended some excavations in the chalk, in which several pits or shafts of various depths had been sunk, and ultimately filled in with a black soil containing numerous remains of Roman and Roman-British pottery, including fragments of Samian ware, together with animal bones, as of the hare or rabbit, &c., with shells of the mussel and oyster, and a few fibulæ.

These pits or wells, as they were called, were supposed by Mr. Diamond to have been formed for the reception of the ashes of the dead after cremation.[1]

In a letter which this discovery gave rise to, the writer, Mr. James Puttock, re-states his opinion that Ewell was the station called *Canca* in the list of Roman towns recorded by the anonymous Geographer of Ravenna. He also mentions his having seen many Roman coins which had been found dispersed near the church at Ewell, and refers to a communication made long ago to Mr. Bray, in which he expressed his belief that the Roman road from Sussex through Ockley and Dorking was continued from Pebble Lane, above Leatherhead Downs, to Ewell, towards which it directly points, and not towards Woodcote, as conjectured by other antiquaries.[2]

THE DOOMSDAY SURVEY

Ewell is thus described in the Doomsday Book:-

> "The King holds *Etwelle*, in demesne. In the time of King Edward, it was assessed at 16 hides wanting 1 virgate; now at 13½ hides, at firm. The extent of the arable land is not specified.

One carucate is in demesne; and forty-eight villains, and four bordars, have 15 carucates. There are two mills, at 10s., and 14 acres of meadow; a wood yielding one hundred swine, and eleven swine for herbage.

In the time of King Edward the manor was valued at £20; subsequently at £16; and now at the same, though it yields £25.

The men or jurors of the Hundred declare that 2 hides and 1 virgate, which belonged to the manor in the time of King Edward, have been detached from it, the Bailiffs having appropriated the land to their friends; as they did likewise a tract of wood and one croft.

To this manor pertains the church of *Lered* [Leatherhead], with 40 acres of arable land, valued at 20s., held by Osbern de Ow."

1. Similar pits have been met with in the Isle of Thanet, Winchester, Chesterford in Essex, and other places. The depth of those at Winchester varies from 30 to 40 feet, and contained rich black mould, including bones and other animal matter, intermixed with fragments of pottery, and occasionally a perfect vase. Those at London, in the neighbourhood of the Roman way in Great Eastcheap, contained sundry vessels of domestic pottery, horns of goats, sheep, &c., and were thought by the late Mr. Alfred Kempe to have been the "*cesspools* of the Roman houses erected near the highway."

2. In a paper on the "Roman Roads and Stations of the Regni," in the *Gentleman's Magazine* for September, 1841, pages 260-2, by Mr. Puttock, the writer infers that the two Roman roads which ied from London to the southern coast, viz. the one to Arundel, the *Anderida* of the Romans, the other to Shoreham, *Portus Adurni*, were not made until the end of the fourth century: they commenced, it is presumed, at or about Newington. The first station on the latter road is thought to have been at Croydon, the supposed *Anicetis* of the Ravenna Catalogue; the second, namely, *Meiezo*, or *Moiezo*, at Merstham. Of three other towns mentioned in the same list Mr. Puttock places *Morionio* at Kingston-upon-Thames, the Moreford of the Saxons; *Ardaoneon* at Guildford; and *Leucomago* at Lewes in Sussex.

THE MANORS OF EWELL

THE MANOR OF EWELL

The superiority of the manor of Ewell remained vested in the Crown until the reign of Henry II, who, not long after his accession, gave lands here, valued at 43s. a year, to Jordan de Blossville. These lands were rated at half a knight's fee, and the owners paid aids and scutage accordingly, in the time of Henry III and in 7 and 15 Edward I (1278-9 and 1286-7), but no notice of these lands occurs subsequently to the date last mentioned.

Henry II also gave a rent of 43s. 3½d. a year in Ewell to Maurice de Creoun, which, in the early part of the reign of Henry III, had descended to Almeric de Creoun, who in 1223 had seizin of £4 per annum in lands in Ewell. His heir, Maurice de Creoun, a knight of Anjou, in 1272 granted all his hereditary right in Ewell, and in other lordships in this county, to Sir Robert Burnel, Knt., and his heirs. The further descent of the property cannot be satisfactorily determined, but Mr. Manning conjectured that the manors of Fitz-Niel and Rookesley, in this parish, may have originated from the royal grants to De Blossville and De Creoun.

The same king, by charter dated at Winchester in 1218, gave to the Prior and Canons of Merton "all his property in Ewell, with all its appurtenances, in *frank almoigne*, with soc and sac, toll and team, infangthef, hamsoken, and all liberties and free customs, and their acquittances, in wood and in plain, and all other places whatsoever, free and quit of shire and hundred court pleas, plaints, geld, and Dane-geld, hidage, scutage, aids, and all customs and secular services, in like manner as any church in England most quietly and freely holds, and in like manner as that land itself stood discharged and acquitted while it was parcel of his own proper demesne."

In the ensuing year Pagan, Sheriff of Surrey, discharged himself at the Exchequer for the lands thus alienated from the Crown, stated to have been of the annual value of £17 17s., of which the Canons of Merton were then in actual possession of one-half, viz. £8 18s. 6d. In 14 Henry II (1167-68) the sum of 20s. was levied on this manor towards an aid for the marriage of the King's daughter.

Richard I granted by charter to the Canons of Merton 101 acres of land in Ewell, without impeachment of assart (implying that the grantees might convert the woodland into enclosures of arable or pasture), and quit aids, levies, escheats, &c.

In 36 Henry III (1251-2) the canons obtained a charter of free-warren for themselves and their successors throughout their manor of Ewell and the lands thereto pertaining.

On the suppression of the Priory of Merton in 1538 this manor reverted to the Crown, and it was annexed by Henry VIII to the newly erected honour of Hampton Court.

Queen Elizabeth, by letters-patent dated 1563, gave Ewell, together with the manor of Wights, to henry Fitz-Alan, Earl of Arundel, whose daughter and coheiress, Joan, was married to John, Lord Lumley, who died in 1609, seized of the manor of Ewell and other estates in Surrey.

Lord Lumley was twice married, but leaving no issue, his sister Barbara became his heiress. She married Humphrey Lluyd (or Lloyd), of Denbigh, a learned Cambrian antiquary, who died about 1570, after which she became the wife of William Williams. Her son, Henry Lloyd, succeeded to the estates of his uncle, Lord Lumley, and from him this manor, with other property, descended to his great-grandson, Robert Lumley Lloyd, D.D.

In 1723 Dr. Lloyd presented to the King a petition to be admitted into the House of Peers, in right of his descent from Ralph, Baron Lumley, who had been attainted of treason for rebellion against Henry IV in 1409, and whose attainder was reversed in 1461 in favour of Thomas de Lumley, his grandson. However, George, son and heir of John de Lumley, who held the barony in the reign of Henry VIII, having been engaged in the insurrection which took place in the north of England in 1536, in consequence of the suppression of the monastic establishments, he was, with several other persons of rank, executed and attainted; and though his son was restored in blood by Act of Parliament in 1547, and admitted to the dignity of a Baron, it was with limitation to his heirs male; consequently Dr. Lloyd, being descended from a sister of that nobleman, could have no legal claim to that title, and his petition was rejected.

He subsequently obtained the rectory of St. Paul's, Covent Garden, London, and dying without issue in 1730, he vested his estates, including Ewell, in trustees, for the use of his sisters during their lives, with remainder in fee to Lord John Russell, afterwards Duke of Bedford.

In 1755 the Duke sold the manor of Ewell to Edward Northey, Esq., after whose decease it descended to his son, William Northey, Esq., to whose nephew, Edward Richard Northey, Esq., it now belongs.

THE MANOR OF BOTOLPHS

The manor formerly called BUTTAILES, or rather BATTAILES, and now BOTOLPHS, parcel of the manor of Ewell, was granted by Henry I to Wm. de Battaille, the grantee rendering to the King the accustomed rents and services.

The descendants of Wm. de Battaille held lands in Ewell until the reign of Henry III, and probably at a later period; but the subsequent descent of the estate cannot be distinctly traced until about the time of Henry V, when it was held by Thomas Hayton, whose daughter and heiress, Agnes, married Thomas, second son of Nicholas Carew, Esq., of Beddington, who thus became possessed of it. He died in 1430, leaving three daughters his coheiresses, one of whom, Joan married Wm. Sanders of Charlewood, whose son and heir, Henry, became proprietor of the entire estate. His grandson, Nicholas Sanders, in 1581 suffered a recovery of the manor, and dying in 1587, he bequeathed it to his son, Sir Nicholas Sanders, Knt., who in 1638 conveyed Buttailes in perpetuity to Thomas Turgis, Esq., M.P. That gentleman or his son, of the same name, bequeathed the manor of Buttailes to his relative, William Newland, Esq., who dying without male issue in 1783, his three daughters became his coheiresses.

In 1765 the estate was sold by their representatives to Anthony Chamier, Esq., M.P., of Epsom, who, leaving no issue at his death in 1780, devised the manor of Buttailes, and other estates in the same parish and in the parishes of Long Ditton and Thames Ditton, to trustees, to the use of his widow for her life, and after her decease to his nephew, John des Champs, and his issue, with remainders to his nieces and others.

In 1784 the devisees of Mr. Chamier joined in a sale of this manor, and those of Fitz-Niel and Rookesley, to Thomas Calverley, who died in 1797, when these estates descended to his son, Thomas Calverley, Esq., of Ewell Castle. That gentleman died in 1842, and was succeeded by his nephew, Hector William Bowen Monro, Esq. The manor of Ewell has since passed to the Northeys, of Woodcote House, Epsom.

THE MANOR OF FITZ-NIEL, OR FITZ-NELLS

Lands and rents in the parish of Ewell belonged to Sir Robert Fitz-Neele, or Fitz-Nigel, in the reign of Edward II; and from the Escheats of 5 Edward III, (1331), it appears that Robert le Fitz-Neele (probably the same person) died seized of 100 acres of arable land and 4 acres of meadow, held of the Prior and Canons of Merton by the service of 15s. a year, and of 100 acres of arable and 2 or meadow, held of Thomas de Codington by the service of 10s. a year, and also of 50 acres of arable, and three water mills, held of the Abbot of Chertsey by the service of 6s. 8d. a year; all which, being valued at £7 17s. 4d. a year, he held for life, by the courtesy of England, after the death of Agnes his wife, of the inheritance of Grace, her daughter and heiress, and which Grace was the next heir of the said Robert, and then thirty years of age.

It seems probable, from a comparison of deeds of 8 and 17 Edward III (1334-5 and 1343-4), referred to by Mr. Manning, that this Grace was the daughter of Agnes, wife of Robert Fitz-Neele, by a former husband; that she married Robert, the son of her stepfather by a former wife, by whom she had a son of the same name; and that, outliving her first husband, she became the wife of John de Nowers.

In 15 Henry VI (1114-5) Richard Leversegge released to John Iwardeby and his heirs all his right in the lands and tenements called Fenelles, or Fenelles Land, in the parishes of Ewell, Codyngton, and Ebsham, which belonged to Robert his father.

In 1477 John Iwardeby, Esq., was lord of the manor. In the beginning of the reign of Henry VII the manor belonged to Sir John Iwardeby, or Ewerby, who, by his wife Katherine, daughter and coheiress of Sir Hugh Annesley, of Mapledurham, in Oxfordshire, had an only daughter and heiress, Jane or Joan, whose second husband was Nicholas Sanders, Esq., of Ewell, son of Henry Sanders, lord of the manor of Buttailes.

This Nicholas had by his wife three daughters, to whom the manor descended, and who probably sold it to the family of horde, many persons belonging to which family are interred in the parish church.

In 1662 Thomas Horde conveyed the manor of Finell to Thomas Turgis, Esq., who held the manor of Buttailes, with which it has been since transferred to subsequent proprietors, and now belongs to Augustus William Gadesden, Esq., of Ewell Castle.

THE MANOR OF ROOKESLEY

Though this manor (as before stated) is supposed to have had its origin from a grant of Henry II, yet nothing is known with certainty as to its proprietors until the latter part of the reign of Henry VI, when it appears to have belonged to Simon Melbourn, Esq., who in 1459 released to John Merston, Esq., and Rose his wife, and Wm. Merston his nephew, all his right and title to the manor of Shaldeford, otherwise called Rookesley, in the parish of Ewell.

In 3 Henry VIII (1511-2) an inquisition took place on the death of William Merston, when it was found that he had held the manor of Horton, and lands in Ewell and Epsom (which probably included this estate), and that Joan and Ursula were his daughters and coheiresses.

The property has since been held by the families of Warham, Turgis, Chamier, Calverley, Monro, &c.

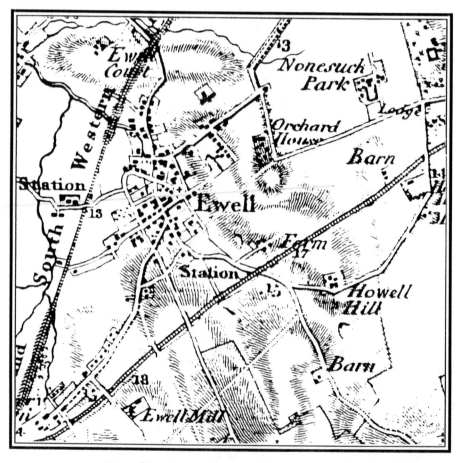

Map of Ewell and the surrounding area c. 1860
with railway lines inserted as they existed in 1891

EWELL CHURCH·

There is no notice in the Doomsday Book of a church at Ewell, but it is stated in that record that the church of Leatherhead pertained to the manor of Ewell "ad hoc manerium adjacet *Ecclesia de Leret*."

The manor of Pachesham, in which Leatherhead was included, belonged to Odo, Bishop of Bayeux, to whose court the rector was not amenable; for it appears from a return of the inquest or hundred jury of Copthorne, in the reign of Edward I (1278), that the church of Leatherhead had been built on a small fee belonging to the Crown, which comprised 40 acres of glebe land, and this fee did not form a distinct manor, but the tenants (and among them Osbern de Ow, the rector of Leatherhead) were required to yield their services at the courts of the neighbouring royal manor of Ewell.

THE ADVOWSON

The advowson of Ewell anciently belonged to the abbot and convent of Chertsey, who, *temp.* Richard I, procured a bull from Pope Clement III authorising the appropriation of the benefice, and other proceedings took place; but it was not until after another bull had been obtained from Pope Clement V, in 1308, that the living was appropriated, and then no provision was made for the support of a vicar, the conventual brethren being left at liberty to appoint an occasional minister or curate to perform religious services on such terms as they might think proper.

In 3 Henry V (1415-6) the church of Ewell and advowson of the same were transferred to the King, in exchange for other landed property; and in the following year King Henry granted the advowson to the prior and convent if Newark, to hold on the same terms as their predecessors had held it, and which they continued to do until the suppression of their house in 1539.

Henry VIII annexed the rectorial estate to the honour of Hampton Court, but Queen Elizabeth, by letters-patent dated 1560, gave it, with all its rights and appurtenances (exclusive of the tithes from land within the park of Nonsuch), to Thomas Reve and George Evelyn, and their heirs and assigns for ever, to be held of the Queen's manor of East Greenwich, by fealty, in free socage, reserving out of the issues of the rectory an annual pension of £11 to the Vicar of Ewell; 20s. a year to the Bishop of Winchester; 3s. 4d. to the Archdeacon of Surrey, for his pension, and 9s. 7½d. for procurations and synodals; with 6s. in allowance for the tithes of 148 acres of land belonging to the rectory, lying within the ancient park of Nonsuch, but in the parish and manor of Ewell, and also for the tithes of 142 acres more enclosed in the park, but belonging to the same parish; and 6s. 8d. as the yearly rent of the rectory.

Sir William Gardener, Knt., of Lagham, in the parish of Godstone, on whom the rectory next belonged, gave it by will, dated 1618, to his son William and the heirs of his body; and, in default of such, to his daughter Mary and her heirs and ultimately to the heirs and assigns of the survivor; but he gave the profits of the estate for life to his widow, with the deduction of £50 a year for the education of his son.

William Gardener, the son, died seized of the rectory in 1632-3, in the twenty-sixth year of his age, and his son or grandson, of the same name, sold it in 1690 to Barton Holiday, Esq., by whom it was resold in 1705 to Sir Richard Bulkeley, Bart., of the kingdom of Ireland.

In 1709 Sir William Lewen, Knt., Alderman of London, purchased the rectory of Sir Richard Bulkeley, and held it until his death in 1721-2, having bequeathed it to his nephew, George Lewen, Esq., whose daughter and sole heiress, Susannah, became the wife of Richard Glyn, Esq., an eminent banker, of London.

This gentleman, who was chosen an Alderman of London, and filled the civic chair in 1758, was created a baronet in 1759. He died in 1772, when the rectory descended to his eldest son, Sir George Glyn, Bart., on whose demise in 1814 his eldest son, Lewen Powell Glyn, inherited the title, estate, &c. Sir Lewen, dying unmarried in 1840, was succeeded by his only brother, the Rev. George Lewen Glyn.

Until the grant of the rectory of Reve and Evelyn by Queen Elizabeth the advowson had been held with it, but being then separated, the latter remained vested in the Crown until 1702, when Queen Anne transferred it to George, Earl of Northampton, who sold it in 1703 to Barton Holiday, Esq., the owner of the impropriate rectory, with which it has been transmitted to the Glyn family, the patronage being now vested in the Rev. Sir George Lewen Glyn.

After the appropriation of the living in 1381, the church of Ewell continued to be served by a curate until 1458, when an endowment for the support of a permanent minister or vicar took place, under the sanction of Bishop Wainflete, ratified by the Prior of Newark, who then held the advowson, and it was covenanted that the vicar should have the manse and adjoining garden, with a pension of 12 marks a year. This sum was afterwards augmented to 16½ marks, or £11, as before stated.

Sir William Gardener, impropriator in the reign of James I, gave by will £6 a year to trustees, in augmentation of the vicar's salary, "to some learned and preaching minister, for preaching and expounding on every second Sabbath day, in the church of Ewel," so long as the rectory should continue in the possession of his heirs; but the impropriation having been transferred to others, the bequest has become void.

Lady Brownlow, daughter and coheiress of Sir Richard Mason, of Sutton, and wife of a Lincolnshire baronet, gave a sum of money to be disposed of by the Bishop of London (Compton), for the benefit of the vicarage of Ewell; and with this donation were purchased the tithes of the liberty of Kingswood, in Ewell, and a small farm at Maldon, which was somewhat augmented by an allotment on the enclosure of the common fields there in 1802.

The land in Maldon (consisting of about 16 acres) and two cottages, belonging to the vicarage of Ewell, together with the vicarage garden (consisting of 1 acre and some roods), were exchanged in 1843 for a house, garden, and paddock, belonging to the impropriator, Sir George Lewen Glyn (he being both patron and vicar at the time), the said house and appurtenances to be assigned to the living at Ewell as a vicarage for ever. It adjoins the churchyard on the east.

ST. MARY'S CHURCH

The old church at Ewell, dedicated to St. Mary, was a very ancient structure of flint and stone and consisted of a nave and chancel, a tower at the west end, and a south aisle, opening at the east end into a chapel, erected by Richard Bray in 1529, and which became his burial place in 1559.

In 1848 the church was rebuilt in the early English style. It consists of a chancel and a nave (separated by a screen), aisles, and a square embattled tower at the west end; and several of the windows are filled with stained glass.

THE TOWER OF THE OLD CHURCH

The ivy-clad tower of the old church is still standing, and is used as a burial chapel to the old churchyard.

THE MONUMENTS

There are some ancient brasses brought from the old church, and also a marble effigy of Sir William Lewen, formerly Lord Mayor of London, who died in 1717.

Among the other monuments and tablets in the old church, most of which have been replaced in the new fabric, may be mentioned those to the memory of the Bulkeleys, Glyns, and Reids, Baronets; and also those to the families of the Calverleys, Monros, Dowdeswells, and others.

THE REGISTERS

The Register of Ewell parish commences in 1604, but is defective. In it is the following entry:-

> Mathew Mountagew of Cobham, and Agatha Turner of Leatherhead; their agreement of marridge was three market dayes published in the Market of Ewell, and they were married by Justis March [Marsh] of Darkin, the 3d of July, 1654.

EWELL CHARITIES

There have been several charitable bequests made to the poor of the parish, chiefly in the last century, among the benefactors being Mr. Thomas Brumfield, Mr. Henry Smith, and Mrs. Helena Fendall.

THE VICARS OF EWELL

In the King's books this vicarage, which is in the deanery of Ewell, is stated to be of the clear yearly value of £24, and is discharged of first fruits and tenths. Manning says, "The sum it formerly paid to the King, whenever an entire tenth was granted to him, was 16s."

Vicars of Ewell in and since 1800:-

1 - John Lewes, LL.D. Instituted in 1777.

2 - James Maggs. Instituted in 1802.

3 - A. H. Baillie. Inducted in 1827.

4 - Sir George Lewen Glyn, M.A. Inducted in 1831.